Singing FISH AND *Flying* RHINOS

Amazing Animal Habits

From the Editors of OWL Magazine

Edited by Katherine Farris

Illustrated by Sam Sisco

Greey de Pencier Books

WHAT'S WRONG HERE?

Ever seen a turtle climbing a tree? That's just one of the strange things going on in this farmyard.

How many more mix-ups can you find?

Answers page 46.

3

BEAKS AND FEET

■ The five birds in this puzzle seem to have gone to pieces! Can you put them back together again by writing the correct numbers and letters in the spaces in the clues?

1. I'm a great horned owl. My beak (#___) is sharply curved to tear bite-sized pieces out of my prey. My feathered feet (___) have long, curved talons to grab small animals.

2. I'm a common grackle. I use my sharp bill (#___) for turning over leaves and catching insects. To make walking on the ground easy, my feet (___) have three toes in front and one behind.

3. I'm a white ibis. I probe into mud for crabs and frogs with my long, curved bill (#___). My long legs and widely spaced toes (___) help me stalk prey in the water.

4. I'm a flamingo. With my large, crooked bill (#___) I strain tiny shrimps and other creatures out of the water. My long legs and flat, webbed feet (___) help me walk in shallow water.

5. I'm a black-bellied tree duck. My flat, hook-tipped beak (#___) is great for ripping up water plants. My pink paddle feet (___) help me swim and walk around on the mud.

Answers page 46.

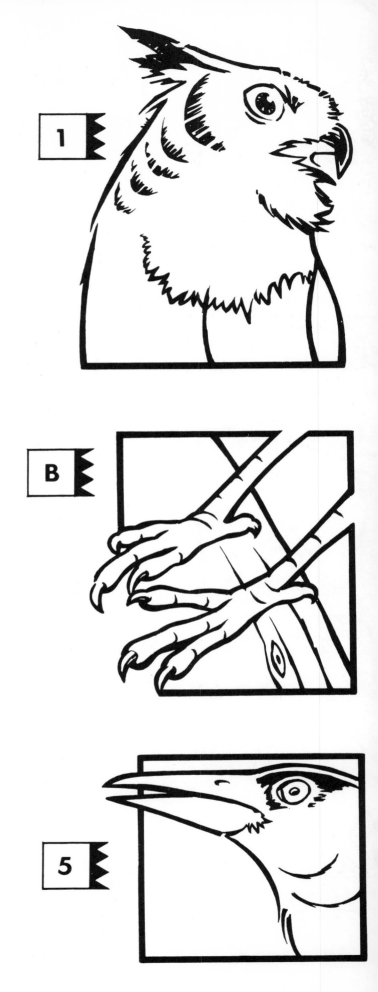

A

2

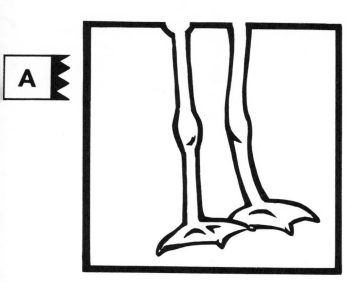

3

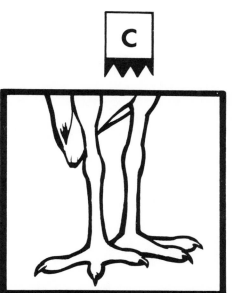

C

4

D

E

5

BIRD'S EYE VIEW

What do you think this albatross would see from high in the air?
What would it see in the water?
How about on land?
Fill in this picture with your drawings of what the albatross would see.

SUPERDADS

All of these animal fathers claim to be superdads, but beware! One of them is bluffing you. Can you guess which one? **Answers page 46.**

1. Lumpfish

I fan my babies with my fins and tail so they won't get dirty. If an enemy threatens them, I attack.

☐ **TRUE**
☐ **FALSE**

2. Marmoset

The only time my babies get off my back is when I hand them over to their mother for feeding. They stay with me until they're three weeks old.

☐ **TRUE**
☐ **FALSE**

3. Emperor Penguin

For two months I stand with my mate's egg on my feet. It's tucked safe and warm under a flap of skin. When the egg hatches, its mother returns from the sea with a belly full of fish for our chick to eat.

☐ **TRUE**
☐ **FALSE**

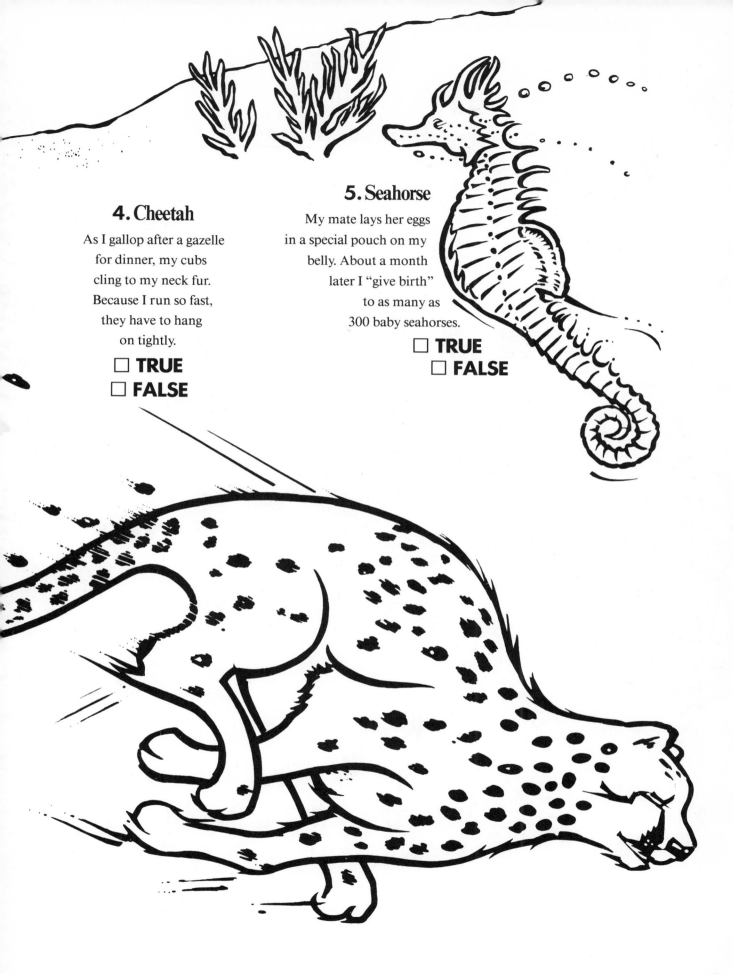

4. Cheetah

As I gallop after a gazelle
for dinner, my cubs
cling to my neck fur.
Because I run so fast,
they have to hang
on tightly.

☐ **TRUE**
☐ **FALSE**

5. Seahorse

My mate lays her eggs
in a special pouch on my
belly. About a month
later I "give birth"
to as many as
300 baby seahorses.

☐ **TRUE**
☐ **FALSE**

ANIMALS IN DANGER

All the clues in this crossword are about endangered animals. Once you've finished the puzzle, you might like to find out more about these animals, and how you can help.

Answers and information page 46.

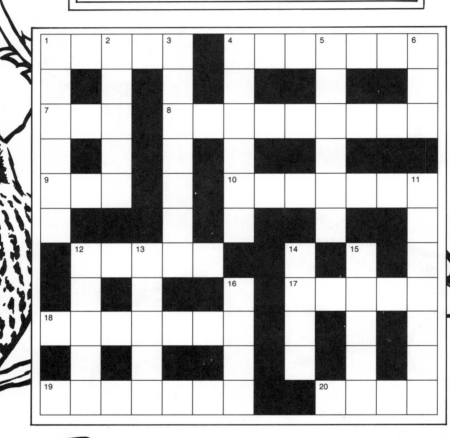

Across

1. Giant pandas are white and _ _ _ _ _.
4. This puzzle is about endangered _ _ _ _ _ _ _.
7. Manatees are called sea cows but unlike cows, they don't make this sound.
8. The area where an animal lives is its _ _ _ _ _ _ _ _.
9. Sea otters have this many babies at a time.
10. This cat is the fastest animal.
12. Sea otters live off the west _ _ _ _ _ of North America.
17. When it's born, the _ _ _ _ _ panda is no bigger than a mouse.
18. What some birds do when the weather turns cold.
19. Moms and dads
20. Beluga whales hear with their tiny _ _ _ _ that are just behind their eyes.

Down

1. Pandas' favourite food
2. Mother and baby pandas live together but other pandas live _ _ _ _ _.
3. What baby cougars are called
4. Cheetahs live in this continent.
5. Which parent looks after baby pandas and baby cheetahs?
6. Cougars hide because they are timid or _ _ _.
11. Peregrine falcons, cheetahs and cougars are all _ _ _ _ _ _ _.
12. The country where pandas live
13. Bird's nest on top of a cliff
14. A leatherback turtle lays more than 100 _ _ _ _ at a time.
15. Black and white and lives in China.
16. Cougars are born in cozy _ _ _ _.

WHO'S THERE?

Make a great animal mask using a paper plate. Be sure to cut the eyeholes large enough so that you can see clearly, then decorate your mask with paint, foil, yarn, markers—whatever! Punch holes at the side and use string or an elastic to tie on your mask. Or, clip a clothespin on the bottom and hold your mask in front of your face.

snail

starfish

WHO'S RELATED?

Look closely at these creatures. All of them are related—except two. Can you figure out who doesn't belong in the family? **Answers page 46.**

squid

octopus

sheep

oyster

clam

sea slug

13

MIGHTY MITES
MEET AN ARMADILLO

Nick, Sophie and Mark Mite are three kids with a big secret: they have discovered a way to shrink to any size they want and grow big again. The Mites are driving through Bolivia with their parents. They get out of the car to stretch and run into an adventure . . .

SEE YOU AT THE BRIDGE IN 10 MINUTES.

DON'T WORRY, MOM, WE WON'T WANDER OFF.

LAST ONE AT THE RIVER'S A ROTTEN EGG.

HEY, THAT'S NOT FAIR! YOU HAD A HEAD START!

BOY, ARE YOU GUYS SLOW!

OW!

TRIP

SOMEONE LEFT THEIR BALL LYING AROUND.

STRANGEST BALL I'VE EVER SEEN.

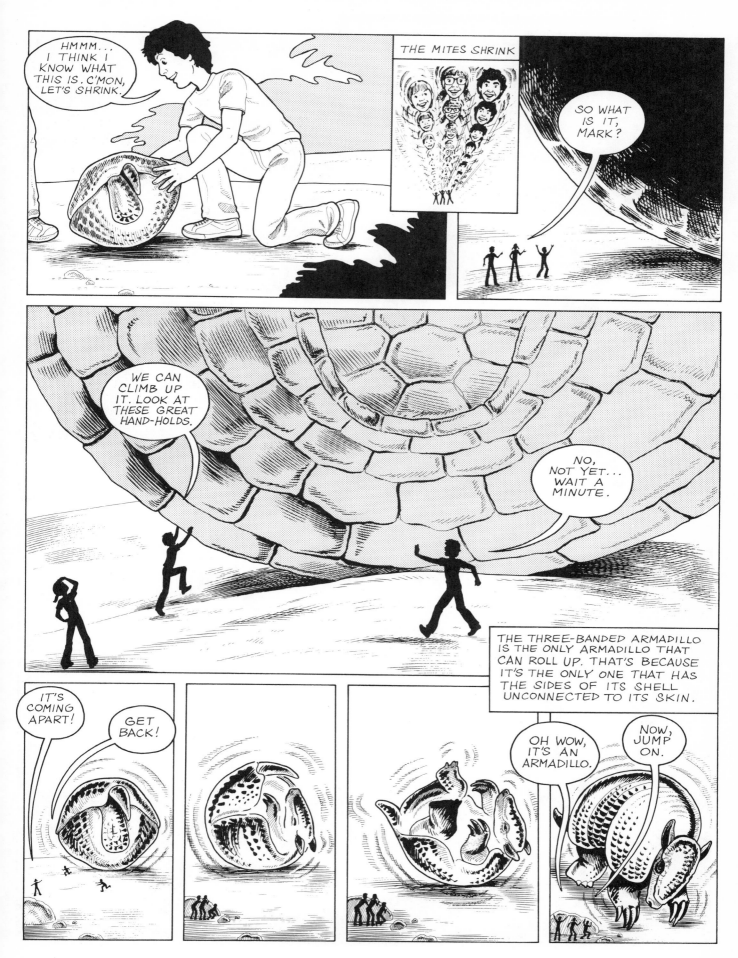

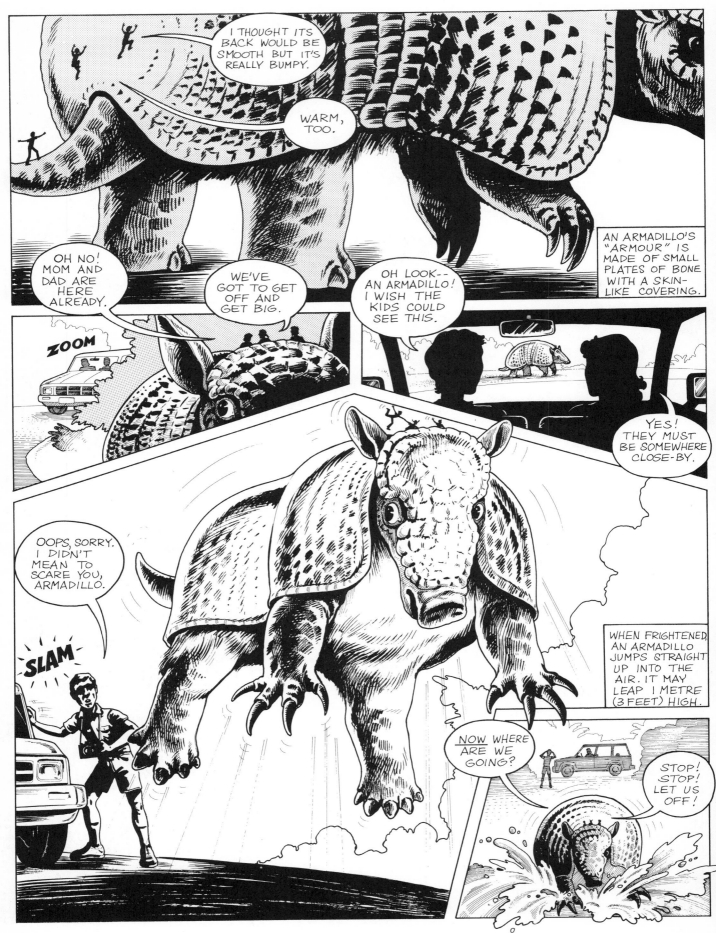

16

FEED ME!

Just like you, every animal has a snack it likes best. Read what each of these hungry animals has to say, then draw its favorite food in the box beside the animal. Fill in the correct name in the space in each clue.

1. In the fall, I wade into the water and snatch salmon as they swim by.

   I'M A _____.

2. In spite of my long tail, I fly from branch to branch and peck at fruit such as avocados and bananas.

   I'M A _____.

3. By flicking out my sticky tongue I can eat as many as 30,000 ants in one day.

   I'M A _____.

4. I'm the biggest animal in the world. Every day I eat tons of tiny shrimp-like creatures called krill.

   I'M A _____.

5. I don't mind prickles and thorns. Sometimes I scrape them off, other times I just bite right through them.

   I'M A _____.

6. I dive into the water, spear a fish, then fly over to a tree and gulp down my meal.

   I'M A _____.

Answers page 46.

SINGING FISH

Test your animal IQ with this true and false quiz.

1. Some people call marine catfish singing fish. These fish sing on summer evenings and their chorus sounds a bit like a coffee percolator at full boil.

☐ TRUE
☐ FALSE

2. The leatherback turtle weighs up to 750 kg (1,500 lb) and has a shell as big as a single bed.

☐ TRUE
☐ FALSE

3. A baby giraffe drops 2 m (6½ ft) into the world when it's born.

☐ TRUE
☐ FALSE

4. The horseshoe crab is the only creature on earth that chews its food with its legs.

☐ TRUE
☐ FALSE

5. When it's born, a baby giant panda is no bigger than a mouse.

☐ TRUE
☐ FALSE

Answers page 46.

HANDS DOWN

Put your hands down here to find out how you size up to these animals. They are all drawn lifesize and are the smallest known animals of their kind—except one! Can you find the animal that is the *biggest* of its kind?

Answers page 46.

BEE HUMMINGBIRD

BUMBLEBEE BAT

STRIPED MUD TURTLE

DWARF BLUE BUTTERFLY

PYGMY MARMOSET

LEAF-CUTTER BEE

DWARF GOBY

PYGMY SHARK

ELF OWL

POISON ARROW FROG

PYGMY MOUSE

THREAD SNAKE

ARBORESCENT OCTOPUS

23

DRAW
A HOME

You've never seen a creature quite like this one. Not only can it climb trees, fly long distances and swim, it can also pluck food from deep in the mud, dig a hole for a burrow and build a soft warm nest for its babies. Give this creature a name, then draw a place for it to live.

TOGETHERNESS

What has 32 legs, 8 trunks and eats 48 bales of hay a day? A herd of eight elephants! Like many other animals, elephants live in groups. To find out why some animals live together, match each clue below with the correct picture.

Answers page 46.

1. A hundred pairs of eyes are better than one. With so many of us on the lookout, we can spot danger early.

   WE'RE _____.

2. There aren't a lot of shallow lakes and lagoons filled with tasty crabs, so when we find one we stick together.

   WE'RE _____.

3. We take turns huddling in the middle of the group to stay warm.

   WE'RE _____.

4. Travelling together makes sense. Youngsters who don't know the way can follow the leader, and everyone flies more easily by sticking close to the bird in front.

   WE'RE _____.

5. In our herd, mothers, aunts and grand-mothers care for the young.

   WE'RE _____.

FOLLOW THE TRACKS

Last night this garden had several mysterious visitors. Use the drawings at the bottom of the page to identify each animal's tracks, then play the true and false game to discover what the visitors did.

Answers page 46.

1. A cottontail rabbit ran into the vegetable patch.

   ☐ **TRUE**   ☐ **FALSE**

2. A deer dug up some snow beneath the apple tree.

   ☐ **TRUE**   ☐ **FALSE**

3. A squirrel jumped from a tree onto the woodpile.

   ☐ **TRUE**   ☐ **FALSE**

4. More than one deer visited the garden.

   ☐ **TRUE**   ☐ **FALSE**

5. A deermouse climbed up the bird feeder.

   ☐ **TRUE**   ☐ **FALSE**

6. A deermouse escaped from an owl and hid in the woodpile.

   ☐ **TRUE**   ☐ **FALSE**

7. A cat sat behind a tree stump.

   ☐ **TRUE**   ☐ **FALSE**

8. An owl sat in a tree.

   ☐ **TRUE**   ☐ **FALSE**

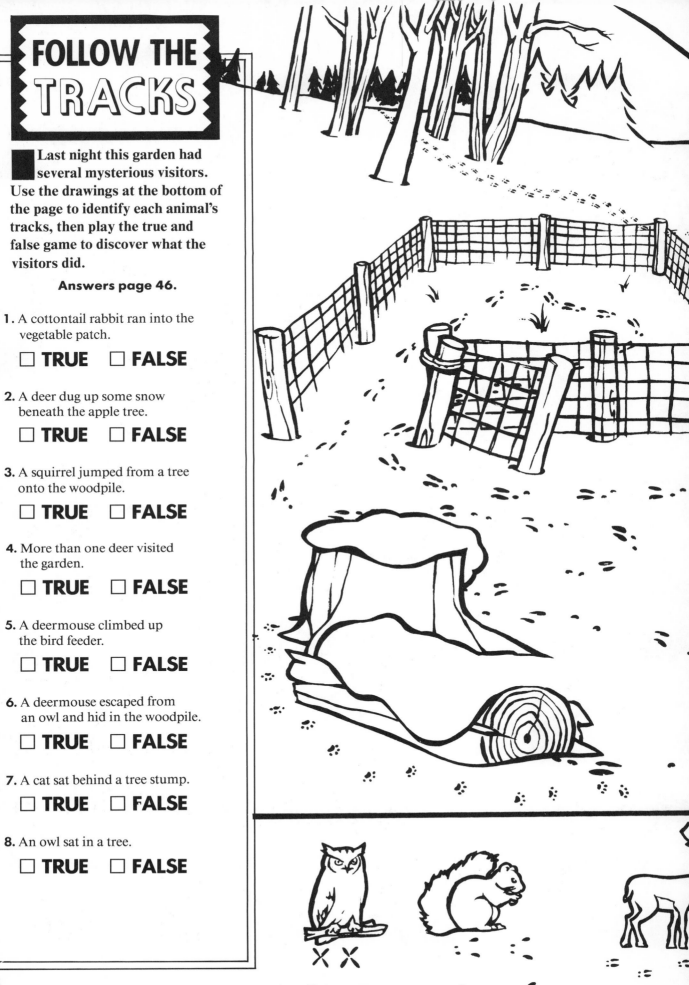

UP TOP

There's lots happening in this pond—both on and under the water. Add to the picture what you would see if you looked under the surface.

DOWN BELOW

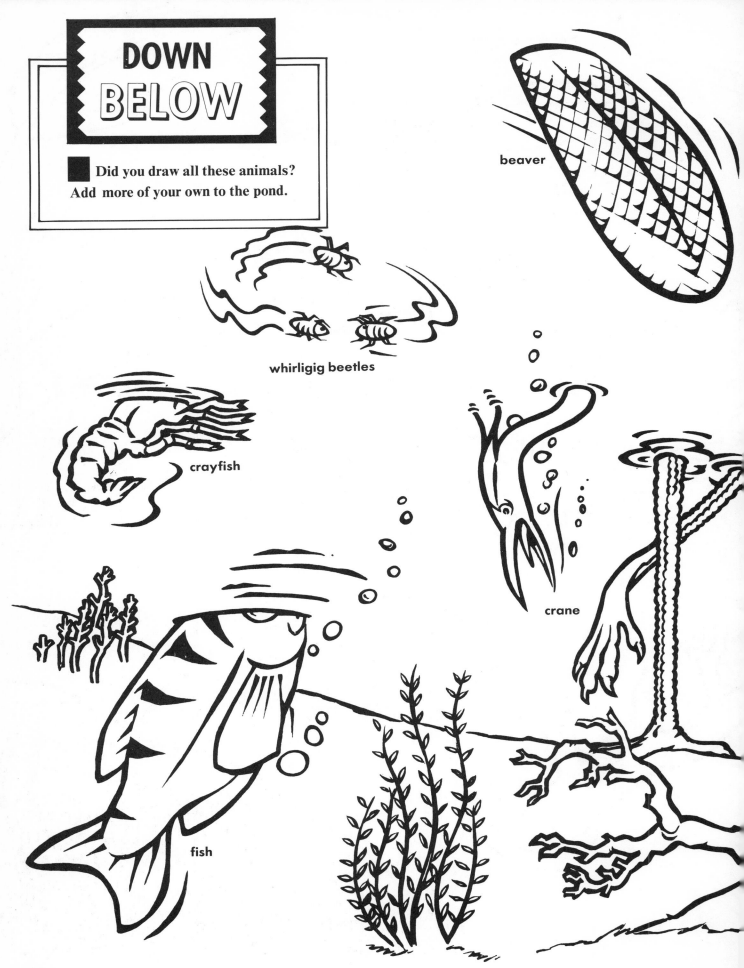

■ Did you draw all these animals?
Add more of your own to the pond.

beaver

whirligig beetles

crayfish

crane

fish

mallard duck

kingfisher

muskrat

33

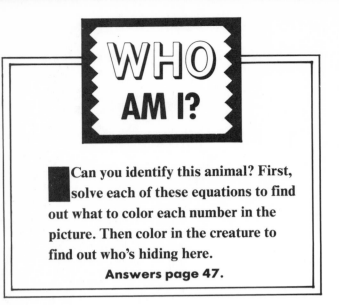

WHO AM I?

Can you identify this animal? First, solve each of these equations to find out what to color each number in the picture. Then color in the creature to find out who's hiding here.

Answers page 47.

PURPLE $= 5 + 3 - 6 =$ _____

BLUE $= 6 - 5 + 3 =$ _____

GREEN $= 2 \times 3 - 1 =$ _____

RED $= 10 \div 2 + 1 =$ _____

YELLOW $= 3 + 7 - 2 =$ _____

BLACK $= 7 \times 2 - 4 =$ _____

RUN, RABBIT, RUN

To protect themselves from predators, snowshoe hares make a maze of tunnels in bushes. Help this hare through the maze safely by avoiding its enemies.

FINISH

FISHER

GREAT HORNED OWL

COYOTE

RED FOX

LYNX

START

PIN THE TAIL

Uh-oh! These animals have lost their tails. Find and draw the missing tail on each animal, but be careful! One of these animals doesn't have a tail. **Answers page 47.**

E

F

A

C

B

D

G

COTTONTAIL RABBIT ☐

CHIPMUNK ☐

ELEPHANT

KANGAROO

GUINEA PIG

WHALE

PEACOCK

SPIDER MONKEY

GOBBLE AND CRUNCH

All the words hiding in this wordsearch are about eating. Find and circle the words in the list below—they're hidden across, down, diagonally and backwards in the puzzle. **Answers page 47.**

```
C R U N C H F T T G R A B
S A R M C H A S E O E A E
T T M T P E A R S B M N R
A U A O M F E N O B E I R
L C H J U M P P O L W A I
K C I L F F S O A E T R E
Y R E P P I L S T C B T S
E S W A L C I A E I S S T
L E A V E S T N G P N E C
D Y D K Y G H M E E O R E
D E C L I B E A K E L A S
A E F D S N R O H T A E N
P R I C K L Y L I A T T I
```

ARM	CRUNCH	HOP	SLIPPERY
BAMBOO	CUT	INSECTS	SLITHERY
BEAK	DIG	JUMP	SPEAR
BERRIES	ESCAPE	LEAVES	STALK
BIG	EYES	MEAT	STRAIN
BONE	FAST	NECTAR	TAIL
CAMOUFLAGE	FLICK	PADDLE	TALONS
CATCH	FLY	PEARS	TEAR
CHASE	GOBBLE	PECK	THORNS
CLAWS	GRAB	PRICKLY	WET

Now, moving in order from left to right and then top to bottom, write the letters you didn't use in the blanks to read a secret message. ___ ___ ___ ___ ___!

38

FLYING RHINOS

The world is full of strange animals, some so weird that it's hard to believe that they really exist. In fact, some of the creatures on these pages don't exist. Can you guess which are real and which ones are bluffing you?

Answers page 47.

1. The Rhinoceros Hornbill of Asia

Some call me a flying rhino because of the big horn on my bill. I use it to make loud squawks to chase other birds from my territory and scare predators like snakes and monkeys. My bright orange horn is filled with hollow air spaces so it's very light.

Am I bluffing you?
☐ YES ☐ NO

2. The Nebduk from Russia

I live on the wind-blown steppes of central Europe where I use my odd-looking horns to dig for grass under the snow. My nostrils point downward so that sand and snow can't blow up my nose.

Am I bluffing you?
☐ YES ☐ NO

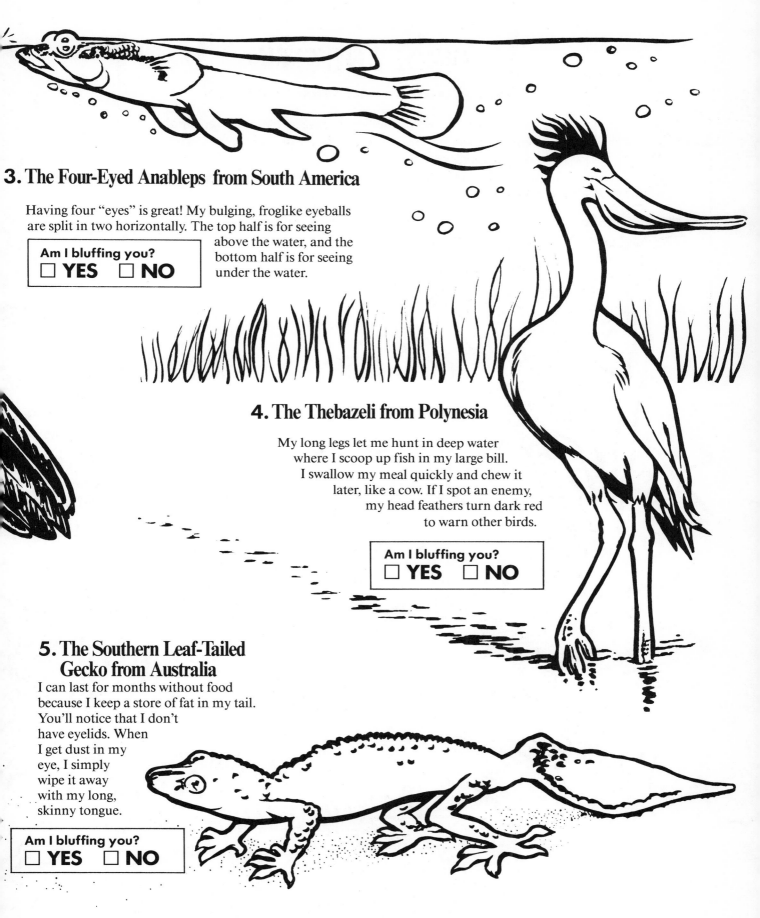

3. The Four-Eyed Anableps from South America

Having four "eyes" is great! My bulging, froglike eyeballs are split in two horizontally. The top half is for seeing above the water, and the bottom half is for seeing under the water.

Am I bluffing you?
☐ **YES**   ☐ **NO**

4. The Thebazeli from Polynesia

My long legs let me hunt in deep water where I scoop up fish in my large bill. I swallow my meal quickly and chew it later, like a cow. If I spot an enemy, my head feathers turn dark red to warn other birds.

Am I bluffing you?
☐ **YES**   ☐ **NO**

5. The Southern Leaf-Tailed Gecko from Australia

I can last for months without food because I keep a store of fat in my tail. You'll notice that I don't have eyelids. When I get dust in my eye, I simply wipe it away with my long, skinny tongue.

Am I bluffing you?
☐ **YES**   ☐ **NO**

UNDERWATER
HIDE AND SEEK

In the warm waters of the South Pacific, many fish and crabs depend on camouflage for safety. Some are strangely shaped so they look like underwater plants, while others have weird growths that make them look like rocks. Some even change color so they blend in. Can you find the 14 fish and crabs around this coral reef?

Answers page 47.

CREATE A CREATURE

Now that you've met so many incredible animals, try drawing one of your own. Here's a pond for it to cool off in, flowers filled with nectar, bushes covered with berries, insects to catch, shrubs to hide in and even a warm hollow to sleep in. What real or imaginary animal do you think would live here?

ANSWERS

WHAT'S WRONG HERE?, *page 2-3*

Turtles don't climb trees.

Bats don't live inside turtle shells.

Geese make their nests on the ground, not in trees. They also sit right on top of their eggs to keep them warm.

A horse has a long tail and ears that stick up.

Penguin chicks would follow an adult penguin, not a rooster. And penguins live in Antarctica, not in a barnyard.

Pigs' tails are short and curly, not long and hairy.

Rabbits don't swim and their tails are stubby and furry rather than long and skinny.

Barnyard turkeys have been bred to have big heavy breasts full of turkey meat for us to eat. While this makes them tasty, it also makes them too heavy to fly. Wild turkeys can fly, but not very far.

Hummingbirds sip nectar from flowers. Their beaks aren't built for eating fish.

A cow's horns don't curl. They just curve upwards.

Baby owls eat mice, not flowers.

But there is one thing that is right in this picture: baby ducks do ride around on their mother's back. This protects the ducklings from enemies under the water that could snatch swimming babies away.

BEAKS AND FEET, *page 4-5*

Great horned owl, beak 1 and feet D;
Common grackle, beak 5 and feet B;
White ibis, beak 4 and feed C;
Flamingo, beak 3 and feet A;
Black-bellied tree duck, beak 2 and feet E.

SUPERDADS, *page 8-9*

The cheetah is the bluffer. Cheetah cubs are raised and taught to hunt by their mother.

ANIMALS IN DANGER CROSSWORD, *page 10-11*

Across: 1. black, 4. animals, 7. moo, 8. territory, 9. one, 10. cheetah, 12. coast, 17. giant, 18. migrate, 19. parents, 20. ears.

Down: 1. bamboo, 2. alone, 3. kittens, 4. Africa, 5. mother, 6. shy, 11. hunters, 12. China, 13. aerie, 14. eggs, 15. panda, 16. dens.

WHO'S RELATED? *page 13*

The starfish and the sheep are not part of this family. All the others are mollusks. Mollusks don't have backbones, instead they have two identical sides. Some mollusks have shells, some don't. Most have a special rasping tongue that gathers food and tears it up. Some mollusks, like the octopus, live in the deep ocean and some, like snails, live in gardens and fresh-water ponds. Some are no bigger than 2 mm, but others, like the giant squid, stretch in at 22 m. Some mollusks stay in one spot for their whole adult life, others like garden slugs and river clams move around slowly, while squids swim about to find food. Some land snails live for years in the hot desert, others live in thermal springs, others survive the winter frozen into the ice. Some mollusks live in dark caves, others live under enormous pressure at the bottom of the ocean.

Common starfish, or sea stars, are from a family called echinoderms. They walk on hundreds of little feet that line their arms. When a starfish gets hungry, it turns out its stomach and chomps on both plants and animals, digesting its lunch before it pulls its stomach back in.

Sheep are mammals. And unlike the other animals on this page, they will do anything to avoid water. Even if a pond only a few centimetres deep, sheep will try to find a way around it. The only time sheep do paddle around in water i when they are put into dipping baths. And then it's only because they have n choice! These baths (sheep dips) contai a special solution that helps to kill mite fleas and ticks that burrow in the sheep wool and skin. When it's time to get ou the sheep gladly paddle over to the edg and haul themselves out.

FEED ME! *page 18-19*

1. bear, 2. quetzal, 3. anteater, 4. blue whale, 5. land iguana, 6. kingfisher

SINGING FISH, *page 20-21*

They're all true!

HANDS DOWN, *page 22-23*

The leaf-cutter bee is the biggest know bee in the world.

TOGETHERNESS, *page 26-27*

1. impalas, 2. flamingos, 3. emperor penguins, 4. snow geese, 5. elephants

FOLLOW THE TRACKS, *page 28-29*

1. True, 2. False, 3. True, 4. False, 5. False, 6. False, 7. True, 8. False

WHO AM I? *page 34*

Did you guess that you colored a king vulture? It lives in tropical forests in Central and South America and its strong, hooked beak isn't all for show. The vulture uses it to tear apart meat, and to help sniff out dead animals in the forest, where it's hard to see very far. It has bald feet just like its head. That way it doesn't get messy feathers when it eats. The vulture also has a pouch for storing food, and a wing span that's almost as wide as a small car is long!

PIN THE TAIL, *page 36-37*

Cottontail Rabbit, C; Chipmunk, F; Elephant, B; Kangaroo, G; Whale, D; Peacock, A; Spider Monkey, E. The guinea pig has no tail.

GOBBLE AND CRUNCH, *page 38-39*

The secret message is FEED ME!

FLYING RHINOS, *page 40-41*

The Thebazeli and the Nebduk are bluffers.

UNDERWATER HIDE AND SEEK,
page 42-43

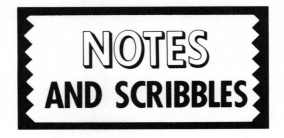

NOTES AND SCRIBBLES